MW01484542

Disclaimer

The information in this book is for educational purposes only. Leveraged trading carries a high level of risk and is not suitable for all market participants. The leverage associated with trading can result in losses which may exceed your initial investment. Consider your objectives and level of experience carefully before trading. If neccessary seek advice from a financial advisor. Never trade with funds you cannot afford to lose.

Copyright Notices

Table of Contents

Introduction

Another price pattern book? Shall I start with some ink stains and interpret those instead? Nope, because what I am about to write in this book are not 'chart' patterns - the are 'price' patterns.

Let's get straight to the point.

What the difference between chart patterns and price patterns, you ask?

The difference is with 'chart patterns' usually go something like this:

"If you see a 'flying dragon crapping under a tree' pattern, it's a sell!"

Yes, it's a sell. A hard sell. Whoever tries to sell you anything based on discretionary chart patterns is usually a failed trader turned salesman. They tend to email you every single day with hot air 'easy money' strategies. What a load of nonsense.

I've worked as a professional prop trader for three different companies and I currently a fintech software development company with a small trading department - and I've never ever heard a single profitable person use chart patterns for their trading decisions.

What they do use is usually a close variation of the following scenario:

"Federal Reserve just raised the interest rates (aka the rate hike), so I am expecting an increased demand for the USD over the next few days/weeks. Therefore I will look at a swing extreme on the Weekly/Daily chart and then wait for the bullish price action pattern to appear before going into my trade to express my macro view of long US Dollar."

So who am I and what makes me qualified to write books like these? My name is Deeyana Angelo and I am a reasonably well-known trader based in London, UK. I hold a Level 4 qualification from Chartered Institute of Securities and Investments (CISI), although I no longer pay for their yearly membership to use ACSI as a suffix after my name. This qualification is equivalent to Series 3 and Series 5 in the USA.

Since 2013, I have carved out a career as a contracting prop trader for three different companies in the USA and UK. Few years back I decided to stop trading for others and instead use some of my money to develop some custom indicators, mainly to take the pain of Excel spreadsheets and manually drawing and calculating my levels. The indicator research and development was done with the help of my trusted CTO James Cater who has over 20 years investment banking experience working for bulge bracket banks as a Technical Software Architect. Our 'Blahtech Indicators' are now well-known to the Metatrader community and we have thousands of users who now have the automation and much needed help with tasks of charting Market Profile, Supply/Demand areas and Average Daily Range. All of this is required to ensure you're entering at swing extremes for maximum profit margins, timing and accuracy. If you wish to check out our products, please see the final page of this book.

Now this book is not about my systematic methodology behind the indicators.

For that, you can head over to my main educational site https://marketstalkers.thinkific.com for our CPD-certified Pro Development Program.

The Program has my face talking at you throughout the course, rather than some dry faceless voiceover - I made this decision because I always used to lose interest with trader videos that only ever have slides and some monotonous-sounding dude talking over them.

Whilst I'm sure that faceless videos of this kind have the potential to be riveting, the reality is that the vast majority of trader education videos are done by blokes who have little to no charisma or a heavy accent that's very difficult to understand. Few exceptions to this are Sam Seiden and Chris Lori, an Olympian bobsled driver turned fx trader. Chris Lori is a prime example of the kind of personality that is required to become a consistently good trader - exceptional self-discipline with an analytical mind, emotionally resilient enough to put yourself under extreme stress both mental and physical to reach the pinnacle of human abilities.

To those who already know me well, I am also a Bodybuilding Champion for several fitness federations in Bikini Fitness category. To date, I've done 9 fitness competitions and came away with 5 trophies, 3 of which were 1st placing. I even competed internationally with WABBA Mr & Miss Universe and finished top 10 in the world. This is the same competition that Arnold Schwarzenegger won back in the 60s.

I am a strong advocate for an active lifestyle for anyone who is seriously considering trading for living. It helps with stress management and also helps to keep your emotional responses under control when things are not going the way you want them to. Trading is a performance skill. In order to succeed you have to learn how to trade by doing it, rather than by watching others. What works psychologically for one person, may not work for you - because you may not have the same issues. Just like you cannot learn to swim by watching a video, you cannot learn to trade by doing the same. You need to get in there, experiment, track data, gather statistics and see what works for you and what doesn't.

In my video courses I give you a detailed working strategy with a clear edge and strong trade locations.
But knowing what makes a strong trade location is only one small piece of the puzzle.

A large part of being successful with the entries is a traders' ability to correctly identify the price action at the Zones of Interest (aka ZOIs for short). And there a huge difference between the voodoo 'chart patterns' and actual 'candlestick patterns. Something that many prospective traders frequently mix up. With grave consequences.

I would like to point out that this book is by no means the most comprehensive collection of reversal candlestick patterns, but merely a study of which patterns have worked for me and my traders in the span of about 10 years trading the live markets through some of the most turbulent times the world has ever seen. Most of these patterns are now algorithmically tested with the help of my Blahtech elves.

Candlesticks, Glorious Candlesticks!

In this book, the full focus will be on the skill of reading Candlestick Patterns. And although these particular candlesticks have nothing to do with actual candles, they will shine a light on your decision making when it comes to trade entries by the time you're done reading it.

Candlesticks should be looked upon as the alphabet of trading or the music notation that enables a musician to interpret a musical piece. Once you learn how to read it, you are able to see the setups with brand new eyes. When combined with trade locations at swing extremes, candlesticks are an invaluable missing link to interpreting the markets correctly.

This is not a book for beginners but rather for intermediate traders who have already been reading the candlesticks for a couple of years. I will not be teaching you what the candlesticks represent and where the open or close is located in the candle representation. I expect you to know this already. If you don't, then this book will go over your head. Instead, I suggest using babypips free school online to learn about the basics of candlesticks and spend a few months getting familiar with reading them in the live markets. The knowledge in this book is something that comes from my own observations and experience from the last 10 years of trading. It also dispels some common myths when it comes to what exactly constitutes a reversal candlestick pattern. This of this book as the practical guide to candlesticks. In Blahtech we also create trading algorithms which are not fully automated as they do require my own human eyes to make a decision on the profit taking, however a lot of the findings in this book is substantiated by our own algorithmic tests. We use a combination of backtests, out-of-sample data and forward tests to determine if an algorithm will perform close to the backtest in the live markets. As such, this book is a rather unique collection of 'dos and don'ts' when it comes to reading price action candlesticks.

So let's begin.

- End of Chapter 1 -

Candlestick Patterns vs Chart Patterns

There is a big thick line between:
1. Candlestick Patterns
2. Chart Patterns

Candlestick Patterns show us valuable information on who is involved in the market and what the price is doing, who is winning and whether the market may be turning, enabling the Trader to make an informed decision about his/her trading idea. They are comprised of 2-4 candles MAX. Anything longer than this and you're either trading on a 2 min chart (tsk tsk tsk) or you're trading outside of regular trading hours when the activity is very low. And you shouldn't be entering a trade at this time anyways! But more on this later in the book.

Figure 1. Four candle consolidation pattern

with a bearish engulf finisher

Chart patterns, on the other hand, are pretty much the same as ink stains from a psychiatrist's office: they are subjective and mostly useless in realtime trading, visible only in hindsight. I've yet to meet a profitable trader who swears that 'The bat in a cave munching on a mouse by the bones of its deceased cousin' is a pattern that brings them profits over and over!

Okay you got me: I'm making fun of the chart patterns. But my point remains: while Candlestick Patterns always allow you to see the potential entry and the necessary stop loss price for your desired trade, Chart Patterns usually have a slew of pictures that involve lots and lots of candles to create shapes of triangles, diamonds, bats, sharks, dragons, butterflies, dandruff-reducing shampoo (head & shoulders ☺) to name a few. They also come with complete ambiguity as to where you should put your stop loss.

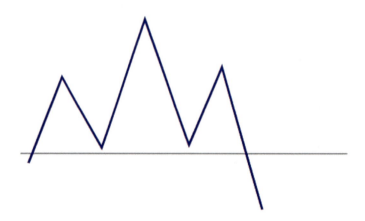

**Figure 2. Head & Shoulders Pattern –
Is the market trying to tell me something?**

They are very arty and fun in hindsight, but realistically these patterns are super-subjective and very improbable when it comes to practical use. And highly impossible when it comes to creating a systematic, mechanical trading system.

Even if you're trading manually, you must strive to be as robotic as possible in the following areas:
1. Choice of trading locations
2. Choice of price patterns that show you the entry
3. Size of stoploss in pips/ticks
4. Duration of your trades
5. Expectation of profit margin (aka risk/reward ratio)
6. If trading intraday - trading at roughly the same time of day

If you are inconsistent with 1, 2 & 3 the trading numbers will be inconsistent as well. Especially with #2 - if you don't know what you're looking for before you enter a trade, you're in the majority of the retail traders who guess a lot. I must repeat this from the previous two books: we are traders, not seers!

Crystal balls and lucky rabbit feet (from a not-so-lucky rabbit!) should have no place in your trading setups.

Figure 3. Mystic Dee strikes again? Nah just a good skill of reading price action!

Although hilariously, I had a nickname 'Mystic Dee' in one of the prop trading firms I worked at because I kept saying things like: "Watch out for 1839 in SPX, it may bounce from it." For the most part, the price would bounce almost to the tick from my levels, so my colleagues said it looked as if I had some kind of a special power. Nothing further from the truth of course. I am simply extremely good at reading the chart with the respective supply/demand areas and resulting price action around those levels. Any skill that's sufficiently advanced enough will seem like a special power to the outsiders. This remains true for my existing traders and students, especially those who have now spent years with me, honing their skills.

You want to be a constitently profitable trader? Learn what your successful trading entries look like upon pressing that button in real-time markets. This book should help you, regardless of which trading method you use.

And finally, there are certain chart patterns that are a bit of a cross between a candlestick pattern and a chart patterns. I am referring to the Double Tops and Double Bottoms - the only chart pattern that I would ever consider for good trading practices.

- End of Chapter 2 -

Price Patterns on Different Timeframes

Before I jump into showing you which patterns to watch out for and which simply don't work, I would like to address the issue that seems obvious but is frequently forgotten - the choice of which timeframe you're basing your trade entry from.

I am not talking about which timeframe you're doing your analysis from (although you should always start with the highest and work your way down to lower timeframes regardless of whether you plan to hold your trade for 3 months or an hour), but actually talking about whether you're using a 5 minute chart or a 4 hour chart to enter trades.

The simple rule is this: the lower the timeframe, the less reliable the candlestick pattern. Although it's entirely possible to trade from a 5 min chart, there are special rules that must be observed.

A bullish engulfing on a Daily chart is not the same as a bullish engulfing on the 5 minute chart. Why? The first reason is that the

Daily chart has so much more trading that went into creating that pattern, so it's obviously going to mean that many institutional traders had to either buy at those levels or get rid of existing positions (liquidate) in order for the market to move the other way.

On the other hand, on a 5 minute chart you really don't need much buying power to move the market – this is less true in thick markets such as EURUSD or S&P500 but very true in a thin market such as WTI Crude Oil for example.

One of the rules that I like to teach when trading from a low timeframe is that the candlestick pattern you're observing on the low timeframe must be absolutely, unequivocally strong and decisive to matter. I also teach that your stop loss needs to be wider for lower timeframe patterns to make sure you're not taken out because of a whippy next candle. So keep your stops quite a few pips wider if you're entering trades from a very low timeframe.

**Figure 4. Lower timeframe Bullish Engulfing pattern –
the subsequent candle takes out the low of the M5 pattern!**

Whereas, if you see a bullish engulfing on the Daily chart, you are a lot more likely to see another whole day of an up move, once you know how to correctly play the pullback into an engulfing pattern, which is my favourite way to enter the market. I call this entry technique

'The Second Chance' and I teach it in the online program.

Another thing to keep in mind when you're trading on lower timeframes is the time of day you're trading. Although forex and cryptocurrency markets are open on most days - forex 24/5 and crypto 24/7 - you really need to understand the instrument you're trading. This involves knowing the Regular Trading Hours (RTH) for that instrument.

If you're trading EURUSD and you decide you're going to trade after you come home from your day job, it's highly likely that by the time you had dinner with the missus, washed up and put the kids to bed, the RTH for EURUSD has been and gone if you're located in the EU and USA. If you then decide you'll also start trading from a 5 minute chart, you're in for a very long evening with little to no action, only to be stopped out in the morning when the real party begins with massive London volumes for the start of the trading session.

The moral of the story is: if you're trading lower timeframes, please make sure you're trading during the active RTH for that particular instrument.

Another example would be trading WTI Crude Oil outside of NYMEX hours. There may be some movement, but if you attempt to keep a trade through the NYMEX open, don't be surprised if the heavy volumes ahead of the session open followed by the noise of the first hour's trading take you out of the market.

You may face the same problem with lunchtime hours - for London and EU session that's between noon - 2pm GMT and for NY session it's 5pm-6:30pm GMT.

SUMMARY:

The lower the timeframe the stronger the pattern needs to be.

If using a lower timeframe, use a wider stop loss.

For lower timeframe entries ensure you're only trading during the Regular Trading Hours for your chosen financial instrument.

EXAMPLES:

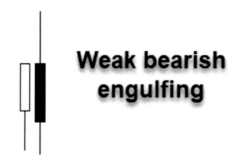

Figure 5. Weak example of a bearish engulfing pattern

In Figure 5. I am showing you a weak example of a bearish engulfing pattern. The reason why this is weak:

- Elongated wicks on either side of the candle, indicating both buyers and sellers are present

- The close of the black candle is just slightly below the open of the white candle, meaning sellers won this round, but not by much

- And finally the close of the black candle didn't close below the low of the white candle

Normally the candlestick studies will tell you that the bearish engulfing pattern is a sell signal, however as you will see throughout this book, not all engulfing patterns are equal. It's all in the context.

If you see this pattern on a small timeframe, anything up to a 4 hour chart, this would not be a valid signal for a short. I would stay out of the market.

However if this pattern appeared on the 4 hour, Daily or Weekly chart, I would consider it as a possible directional signal for a short trade, but for the actual entry I would need the price to go higher into the black candle – somewhere closer to the top quarter of the black candle before I would consider a short purely based on this candlestick pattern.

The reason for this is to try and get a possibility of a good risk/reward ratio on the trade, but really I would expect this pattern to fail, because it screams 'indecision' due to the wicks present and lack of a confident close in relation to the previous white candle.

On the other hand if you see something like this:

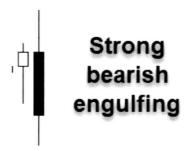

Figure 6. Wicks on both sides here too, but this is a strong bearish engulfing

pattern

this would represent a good sell signal. The wicks on bearish
engulfing is present in both examples on the black candle, but it's
really the white candle that gives this pattern context.

In Figure 5. the white candle is almost equal-bodied to the black one
and the close of the black candle is within the white candle length.

In Figure 6. white candle body is small enabling the black engulfing
candle to not only 'swallow' the entire length of the previous candle,
but to also confidently smash the low of the previous candle,
confidently closing just below the white candle's low. All of these
are signs that there is intent from some large institutional investors
to reverse the price. Whether you saw this on a 5 minute chart or a
Daily chart, it would definitely mean that a sell trade is a very
strong probability.

However if you are trading from a low timeframe, you really want to
look for strong signals like the one in Figure 6, whereas Figure 5
pattern may only work on a larger timeframe for any trend
continuation.

- End of Chapter 3 -

Stop Loss Placements

Practical examples of localized vs non localized stop losses

Where you place your stop loss as a trader can literally make you or break you. So before I go into the pattern-by-pattern studies, I want to make sure you have the understanding of how to obtain the strongest entry in relation to your observed candlestick pattern, but also to ensure you notice whether the pattern is anywhere close to a round number of the instrument you're trading.

What do round numbers have to do with trading? Quite a bit actually!

Algorithms that we're all up against love taking people out of their entries and stops are placed at 'weak' prices.

Practically speaking, as a trader you must ensure that you buy at prices just underneath the round number, after the market dips and breaks the round number. Let's say you're looking at eurusd and you see a candlestick pattern of interest spanning from 1.1518 all the way down to 1.1504:

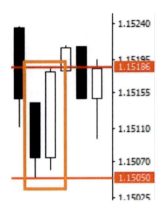

Figure 7. Bullish engulfing on a 15 minute chart,
EURUSD - 2nd Oct 2018 at 9:30am BST

Most inexperienced traders would then enter a trade with the
following stoploss placement:

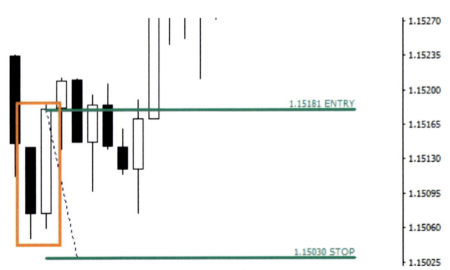

Figure 8. Stop loss placed at 1.1503, just above the round number

This kind of stop loss placement that completely disregards where
your round number is, will generally put your position in danger of
algorithms who just love these kinds of positions. You may get lucky

if you are quite knowledgeable about market timing in relation to Regular Trading Hours and usual behaviours of your chosen instrument. Unofrtunately more often than not, a trader may be correct when it comes to the direction of the trade, only to be taken out of the market when the algorithms pop the round number for some quick profits. And then the trader blames the big bad brokers, instead their own ignorance. So let's lift the ignorance and use this algorithm behavior to our advantage rather than whining about how evil the brokers are, shall we?

Let's think about this logically:

If I'm expecting the round numbers to get popped, I should probably aim to get my entries as close to the round numbers as possible.

Where should I place my stop loss? NOT AT THE ROUND NUMBER!

The clever placement of the trade entry with a very strong stop loss would be:

Long ENTRY anywhere from 1.1495 – 1.1510

STOP LOSS around 1.1470 – 1.1480

As an example here is what that may look like on the chart:

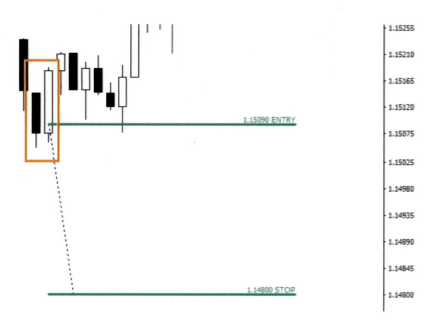

1.15255

1.15210

1.15165

1.15120

1.15090 ENTRY

1.15075

1.15025

1.14980

1.14935

1.14890

1.14845

1.14800 STOP

1.14800

**Figure 9. Clever entry and stop loss placement
in relation to existing bullish engulfing pattern**

By taking round numbers into account when you spot an opportunity for a trade, you can avoid the nail-biting moments of price re-testing the area deeper getting close to your tight stops.

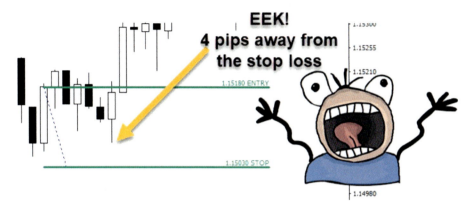

Figure 10. Original stop loss placement may ruin your zen

Nit-picking on pips/ticks when it comes to stop losses leads many a trader to age overnight. So please - make things easier for yourself and before you press that button, ensure that your stop losses are well thought-out.

If you can get an opportunity to go long just under the round number, this is the strongest position you can find yourself in. The opposite is true for short trades: entries above the round number after another move up will be in a great position and largely no hair-pulling moments when the market is testing the levels deeper.

For short trades, I usually try to have my stops around .30 above the round number. For example if eurusd was to move all the way back up to 1.1600, I would aim to place the stops at 1.1632. If the stop loss is a bit large, I may consider using 1.1627.

Obtaining an entry above and below the round numbers may not always be an option, because the markets are organic. However the choice of stop loss placement is always in your control.

Another thing to mention about stop loss placements is to not use a localized low/high of the pattern that has just appeared. By now, most folks know that I trade through my own use of supply/demand levels, which always demands looking to the left of your chart to see where the previous move came from.

I then find the low/high that happened much earlier causing the initial move away. I then wait for these swing extremes to get re-tested and if I see a reversal (or rejection) pattern at the area, I will enter the trade. With this in mind, I dislike using localized stop losses based on the actual newly formed pattern I've observed in real time.

Figure 11. Original Swing Start Area

So if you scroll back through the chart, you can find areas where the original swing started - this is usually what the institutions are seeing through their order books, but if you're skilled enough as a Supply/Demand trader, these areas are perfectly visible without any order books to peer into. Of course, this is a vast oversimplification of S/D trading which I won't go into in this book. I've written two books on the subject and if you're interested to learn my methodology of using S/D and Swing Extremes aka Q Points to trade, please refer to "Market Stalkers: Price Action Trading" and "Market Stalkers: Mastering Day Trading for Income", both books easily available to purchase on Amazon

Quick Section on Interest Rates and Impact of Underlying Currency Pairs Momentum

In this day and age, the golden age of easy trend trading is pretty much long gone. The prices go up and down a number of times over a number of hours and sometimes days, retesting the levels over and over, playing with the trader's confidence making us question the meaning of life itself, before making the actual move away from your area, one direction or the other.

About 10 years ago, pre-recession and hell that followed, any reasonably skilled trader was able to find a trend and then get in at the first available opportunity, allowing the momentum to take the trade in the correct direction. The poor choice of a trade location didn't really matter that much, because the momentum would reward the subpar entry price. However these days traders have to be extremely skilled to profit from the markets.

One reason for this is the lack of interest rate differentials between the countries. Back in the day, something called a 'carry trade' was a big thing: buy the currency of a country with the highest interest rate, hold it for a while and then sell it for insane profit some time later.

You would identify the country with the highest interest rate and pit that currency against a country that has a lower interest rate.

Usually it would be AUD or NZD against the USD or GBP because historically AUD and NZD had interest rates that went anywhere from 8%-13%. Comparatively, these days (it's end of 2018 as I write this) AUD interest rate is 1.5% and NZD stands at 1.75. Since I'm already writing about carry trades, I have to mention the death of JPY carry trade. Japan's interest rates are now in the minus - currently standing at -0.1%. So it's a strange world of global debt we're living in with most countries struggling to keep their economies afloat.

But let's get back to carry trades: cross pairs that had AUD, NZD or JPY were absolute monsters for profits with the interest rate differential of about 5-6% or even more in certain cases. We would frequently see GBPNZD go 400-500 pips in one day as a standard!

Back in the 90s New Zealand had an interest rate of 15% while UK held at 5%. Even after the crash, although there was a less of a differential, New Zealand still held rates at about 5%, while UK went down to 0.25%. Up until a few years ago, this still worked incredibly well for purposes of 'trend trading'. However due to various issues across the Western world and a crisis that threatened a systemic breakdown of the capitalist system as we know it, banks decided to lock down the interest rates in a bid to control their flailing economy. The trick worked, however we are only now seeing a bit of a momentum rebound in the markets at the end of 2018. The momentum is not back like is used to, however it's certainly miles better than it was about a year ago.

If you are planning to trade in the forex markets, please take this into consideration when choosing which fx pairs to trade. Your choice may determine or hinder your success when it comes to pure numbers.

Lack of interest rate differential = lack of momentum. Many retail traders will try to argue that there are some mystical forces at work when it comes to momentum but there aren't.

It's a matter of underlying reasons why the markets move in the first place, with the interest rates driving the demand in any particular currency. There's no secret, only misinformation and people wanting to believe that this is more complicated than it actually is.

- End of Chapter 4 -

Practical Use in Real-Time Markets

This entire section will be about actual candlestick patterns in live markets with my own observations of what works and what doesn't work.

I've come by this purely because of my own trading experience over the previous 10 years. I like to journal each of my observations and then track them over a number of months (even years in some cases) before I make a definite conclusion about the validity of a pattern.

One last thing I would like to say is that a pattern will be stronger if it's located in a relevant swing extreme on higher timeframes or if it's happening at the correct time of day when an intraday price reversal usually occurs.

So if you end up seeing a reversal pattern in the middle of the night on EURUSD whilst you're in London, it's not going to be as relevant as seeing the same pattern at London trading session open.

Likewise, a pattern in the middle of a previously established swing is less relevant than a pattern at a swing extreme or a top/bottom quartile point of a swing move aka Q Point – this is my own proprietary concept which is included in Blahtech SD indicator (available from MQL5.com App Store). If you already own Blahtech SD, pressing letter 'Q' on your keyboard will bring up the Q Point of a timeframe you're currently on. Pressing 'Q' multiple times will jump to the next higher timeframe.

Finally, I will only talk about reversal aka rejection candlestick patterns with no mention of 'continuation' patterns as I don't feel they're that relevant to the trade management once you're already in a trade. There are much better ways to get into a continuation of a trend with Market Profile. Read about them in my vol 2 book.

Engulfing

Let's start with the clearest candlestick pattern of them all: Engulfing Candlestick Pattern.

This can be a Bullish Engulfing or a Bearish Engulfing. Bullish engulfing signals a buy, bearish engulfing signals a sell.

It's a 2 candle pattern that can tell you who is winning. It's by far the most comprehensive rejection pattern that I've used over and over with great conviction and usually has about a 70% chance of working out in most cases. It has an even higher chance when it happens at a relevant area where the beginning of the move first occurred.

Here is what strong bullish engulfing patterns may look like on actual charts:

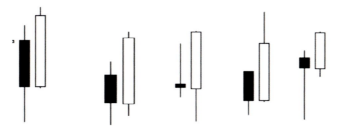

Figure 12. Strong bullish engulfing examples

The first thing to note about an engulfing pattern is that the second candle body completely engulfs the previous candle body. Engulfing patterns appear at the end of a trend. They signal that whoever was in control up until that point is now gone.

There are two reasons why an engulfing pattern appears on the **Daily chart**:

1. It's either that the institutional traders have stepped in

2. Institutions have liquidated their positions, causing the price to move the other way.

The second reason you can usually see on the chart quite clearly, because they usually have a long buying wick like in the last example:

Figure 13. This bullish engulfing appears when institutions liquidate their large positions

Usually these kinds of engulfings will show up on the **Daily chart** ahead of important releases or after a new piece of crucial information has come into focus. On smaller timeframes, they are usually a result of a large options expiry or a portfolio rebalancing for end of day.

The way I usually play the Daily entries for the engulfing is to wait for a pullback into the area where the price crossed over the other way. I call these key levels 'conterminous lines' because they represent a newly formed area of a demand or supply. 'Conterminous' literally means 'to share a common boundary'.

When it comes to price and engulfing patterns, as you are watching the engulfing being created in realtime, at some point the price of the second candle will start to turn around and cross the boundary of the previous candle's open price. So at that point, they look the same – the price goes into equilibrium, into a sideways pattern before continuing to rise, eventually resulting in an engulfing candle. However please note that for an engulfing pattern to become valid, **you must wait for the second candle to close fully.**

If you start guessing and getting excited that you've spotted a bullish engulfing on the chart, one thing that may likely happen is that over the next couple of minutes your potential bullish engulfing candle turns around and rushes down to finish in another black candle, dragging you into a feeling of mild peril.

ALWAYS WAIT FOR THE CANDLE TO FINISH PRINTING ON THE CHART.

Bearish engulfing is the same, only for the sell trades. The bearish engulfing pattern appears at the end of an uptrend.

Examples of strong bearish engulfing patterns:

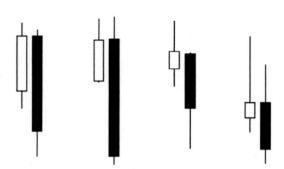

Figure 14. Strong Bearish Engulfing Patterns

There are weak engulfing patterns that don't work as well – they may
bring about a change of trend but the pattern can't be flimsy.

Here is an example of a weak Bearish Engulfing pattern:

**Figure 15. Weak Bearish Engulfing - the black candle body
is almost the same size as the white one**

In Figure 15, not only is the body of the black candle nearly the
same size as the white one, but the black candle failed to make a new
lower low – never a good sign. So although this is a textbook bearish
engulfing, I would only use this to kick of an actual trade if the
pattern was a part of another few candles that consolidated, aka went
sideways and then printed this engulfing.

Similarly, here is a bearish engulfing that doesn't quite close low
enough:

**Figure 16. Lower low, but the close of black candle
is not far from open of the previous candle**

Now let's do some examples of a weak Bullish Engulfing:

Figure 17. Failed bullish engulfing

According to the text books, the definition of a bullish engulfing is
when the second candle body engulfs the previous candle body. Well
the example above does just that, however to me the massive selling
wick on the second candle tell me that the buyers failed to keep the
price up. So therefore, this is a weak bullish engulf and therefore
not valid for trading. This is also widely known as a 'dead cat
bounce'.

And another example of this weak bullish engulf:

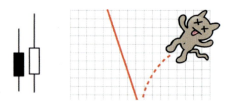

**Figure 18. Dead cat bounce: Similar size candle body,
a selling wick on the second candle**

In fact every time I see this kind of a pattern, I would actually consider it as a great option to go with the trend the next day – to sell the intraday rally! I guess you could call it a continuation pattern, because we assume that the buyers have failed to keep the price up, therefore sellers are still in control.

While I'm on the subject of continuation trades there is something else to keep in mind – in an uptrend, if you see another bullish engulfing, that is not a good entry for a continuation trade in the market conditions today unless there is also a Market Profile Value Area edge at the same spot. And even then, it's only an opportunity for a short-term intraday trade, more of a 'scalp' if you will. I advise against these for inexperienced traders, but for those of us who have lived and traded through these opportunistic intraday moves we are absolutely able to catch them on a regular basis, especially in more liquid products.

But if you're looking to get into a swing trade off the back of a bull engulf after the market stuttered on the way up, there is a high probability that the bullish engulf is way too high in the distribution curve for institutional investors to see the location as a viable entry for a longer-term position trade. In fact, this usually means that the steam is running out. What you really want to be looking for is catching that first momentum of a trend turn. This is what has the largest reward and the lowest risk.

Attempting to catch a trend when it's already on the way is a sure way to keep getting knocked out and frustrated. I've made all my money on trend turns and only a relatively handful of trades on a continuation.

Most of the continuation engulfing trades I used to attempt in my early trading days would end either with a loss or with only a few pips.

The only memorable successful trade I took on a continuation of an uptrend was a Crude Oil trade after an announcement that a war in Iraq has broken out and supply lines have been cut off. I only heard the news relatively late in the London session and I still jumped in on the action after the price had already moved about 150 ticks on the day. But I identified the news as something worth the risk and went in to hold the trade for most of the day, banking about 350 pips which resulted in one of my best intraday trades banking me about 420 pips which at that time made me $32,000 for about 7 hours trade duration.

The rest of my big memorable trades were all done on trend turns, lasting between 16 hours up to around 4 days.

Timing of Patterns

When observing the price in real-time, experienced traders will agree that this is an entirely different ball game than watching the historical chart data. In hindsight, everything is clear!
But when you're sat there, by yourself, watching the prices move up and down, it's easy to lose perspective.

Whenever I start working with new traders, I've noticed that many get excited when the market seemingly starts creating a bullish/bearish engulfing when the new candle begins.

Figure 19. New candle begins, looks like a bullish engulf!

However, I don't like seeing this at the beginning of the new candle. The best engulfings are those that eventually get created towards the end of the candle creation - because it's a lot more likely that the engulfing patterns will hold. Same goes for watching the Daily chart for an engulfing. The earlier in the day it is, the less likely it is that the candle will hold until the end of the day.
If the candle is still new, regardless of the timeframe, there is still a lot of time left on the clock before it prints the final result. The amount of times that a new traders would enter the position without waiting for the candle to print, only to find that a few minutes later, their trade is underwater and the final 'printed', finished candle looks like this:

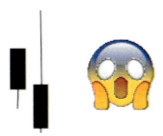

Figure 20. Oh no! Bullish engulfing didn't hold

Therefore: just because a candle looks like an engulfing, it doesn't mean it will hold. So let me repeat this again: *you must wait for the candle close!*

By the way, this goes for *any candle price action pattern you're expecting*.

Consolidation Pattern

Consolidation pattern usually consists of 4 candles. It looks like this:

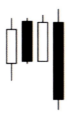

Figure 21. Bearish Consolidation Pattern

Notice that the final candle is a bearish engulfing candle! If you come across 4 candles without that 'engulfing finisher' candle, it's likely that you're looking at a price 'speed bump' rather than a consolidation pattern that you can use as a reversal. Consolidation must have the finisher candle that tells you the market failed to continue and has now decided to reverse direction. This pattern can be used on any timeframe from weekly and daily, all the way down to 30 minute and even 5 minute timeframe.

Some people may ask: isn't any sideways movement a consolidation? Well no. Because the consolidation pattern is characterized by the uniformity of candle bodies. If you have a sideways movement looking like this:

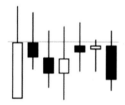

Figure 22. Invalid. Price is moving in a tight range, but isn't a true consolidation pattern

Then it's more likely you're looking at a market that's either outside of Regular Trading Hours or in case you notice this on the large timeframes this usually means it's a quiet season, like summertime or January. This does NOT represent the Consolidation Pattern. In order for the consolidation pattern to be valid it must have the following:

1. Uniform or near-uniform candle bodies, with open and close

prices at/almost the same price
2. It must have an engulfing finisher candle
3. Comprising of about 4 candles as a standard
4. If there is more than 5-6 candles, it's lack of interest

When trading lower timeframes consolidation pattern during Regular
Trading Hours is incredibly important.
I would like to emphasise: *during Regular Trading Hours (RTH)*.

It's so important not to confuse out-of-hours price action as a
potential signal, because the fx markets and crypto run 24/5 and 24/7
respectively. There is a considerable difference in volumes and
relevance of candlesticks patterns depending on the time of day
you're trading them.

If you spot a sideways movement outside of RTH, it's likely that
you're looking at nothing but a lack of movement, lack of interest,
absence of trading.

However, if you happened to spot a consolidation during active
trading hours, this is a very valuable skill to have. Consolidation
of this kind at the right time of day can even be used on a 5 minute
timeframe with great success for those with solid self-discipline.

Consolidation during RTH tells us a valuable piece of information:
that for whatever reason, the price is failing to advance further in
the same direction.

You don't even need to know the reason why. You have all the
information you need:

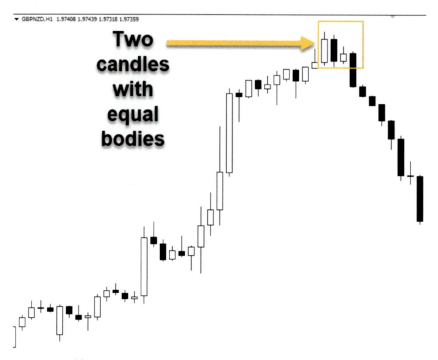

Figure 23. Consolidation with bearish engulfing finisher

In the example above, you see the two candles with almost identical bodies, followed by a third smallish candle and finally a confident engulfing move downwards, signalling the end of the upwards move for the day. This was taken from a 1 hour chart on GBPNZD, an instrument which can be traded pretty much 24/5, since it tends to have an ok range for all three major sessions: Asia, London and New York.

When you're watching the chart and you think you've spotted two candles that have started to consolidate like in the example above, you still must await the engulfing finisher.

Ideally you want the engulfing candle to appear on the same timeframe as the candles that already have an equilibrium. But I advise traders to use the Timeframe Intermix technique: you spot an equilibrium on a

30 min chart but then using time of day plus a 5 minute chart to look
for an engulfing 'finisher' to obtain an earlier/better entry with a
smaller stop loss. Timeframe Intermix technique does take a lot of
experience and calmness to master, so until you've lived through at
least 100 realtime trades where you develop a feel for it, it's
probably easier to start on the same timeframe. I explain this
technique of orienting yourself for intraday trades for best outcome
at the beginning of Level 3 of my Professional Development Program
where I also show a session of my own live trading.

If you are not sure of what exactly to look for whilst switching
timeframes, you may be tempted to go into invalid consolidations,
such as this one:

**Figure 24. Consolidating candles on a 30 min chart,
but no engulfing**

This consolidation failed because ultimately it didn't have an
engulfing finisher candle, showing you the new direction. It was
merely a market pause, probably for lunchtime before continuing in

the same direction.

I myself mix and match timeframes constantly, especially intraday - I flip between them to make sure I am getting all the information available. This is a skill that I've only really mastered in the last couple years, even though I've been working on it for nearly 10 years.

What I do is wait until I notice the consolidating pattern on either 15 or 30 minute chart and then I look for an engulfing pattern on a 5 minute chart.

However I am quite selective over what kind of engulfing I want to see on the low timeframe. I need the low timeframe engulfing candle to do the following:

1. Stop creating lower lows or higher highs
2. Reverse and close the candle outside of the entire consolidating area in the opposing direction

What this looks like on a chart:

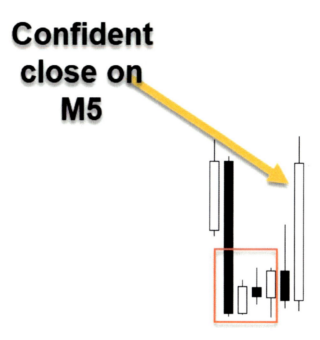

Figure 25. Low timeframe must have a confident move

This is an example of a low timeframe, also showing a previous 4 candle consolidation with a weaker engulfing, however because the first engulfing doesn't come out of the consolidating area and barely scrapes the high of the previous candle inside the marked rectangle, this is simply not enough of a signal that the buyers have taken control. However the final candle shown unequivocally goes higher than the consolidation and closes completely outside of the area. This is of course an extreme ideal example. In the real markets you'll come across less ideal-looking candles, however the bottom line is that you're looking for a strong, confident evidence that the other party have taken over.

SUMMARY:

Consolidation pattern shows you that the price has stopped moving in the same direction, for whatever reason, giving a potential opportunity for a trade in the opposite direction.

The consolidation pattern is comprised of a minimum 4 candles and needs a bullish/bearish engulfing finisher to be a valid signal for trading.

You can mix and match timeframes, however the lower the timeframe, the strong engulfing candle must be. It needs to clear the consolidating area and close confidently outside of it.

Stars – Morning Star, Evening Star, Shooting Star

Stars are beautiful both in the evening sky and on the trading charts.

They can be a pretty good indication that the market has lost steam in the current direction and may be setting up for a reversal.

Morning/Evening Star Pattern is comprised of three candles and has a characteristic 'neutral' candle in the middle:

Figure 26. Evening Star Pattern

Sometimes the middle candle is a 'doji' which is the ultimate 'indecision' candle. However out there in the real world, you'll most likely come across examples akin to the one above in Figure 26. A small candle that seems undecided on whether it wants to go further.

The third candle is usually a strong candle in the opposing direction.

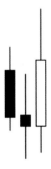

Figure 27. Morning Star Pattern

The third candle doesn't necessarily have to go above the entire pattern, however it does need to be a decent move. I don't like to see any extended wicks on the last candle so here is an example of an invalid pattern:

Figure 28. Still a Morning Star, but suspicious

I wouldn't trust this pattern to be a true reversal because it indicates that the sellers were able to make quite an impact. Meaning they are probably not strong enough to take the price in the opposite direction.

It also means that if you were to scan lower timeframes than the one you're tracking, you'll notice a resistance area (aka supply) that was created when the sellers stepped in.

This means even if the reversal happens, the price will run into the resistance and will take some time to break through it. Therefore, you're looking at a painful trade lasting much longer than it should.

Shooting Stars and Hammers

Many books are quite adamant that Shooting Stars and Hammers are reversal patterns. I disagree.

My experience with them is that if they are a 'stand-alone' candle, they are nothing but an immediate reaction which typically gets retraced and obliterated in the next few candles.

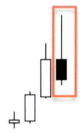

Figure 29. Shooting Star - lonely candle,
not valid for reversal trade

More often than not, they are nothing but a pivotal 'pop' into supply or demand. After they print the 'reaction', the price usually happily continues in the same direction until it completely invalidates the textbook 'reversal'.

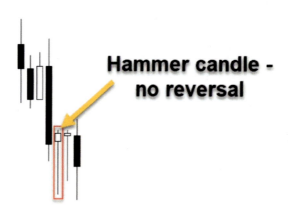

Figure 30. Hammer Candle –
ultimately failed after retracing completely

However, I did find that if the shooting star or hammer are a part of the consolidation pattern or are followed by an engulfing candle to form bullish/bearish engulfing, then they are a valid signal for the trade. But on their own, I've never found them to have a high enough accuracy for a high reward trade in the opposing direction.

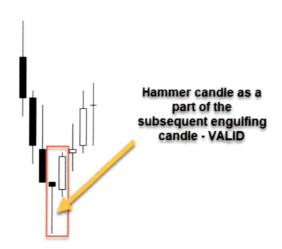

Figure 31. Hammer candle followed by an engulfing –
it's a reversal

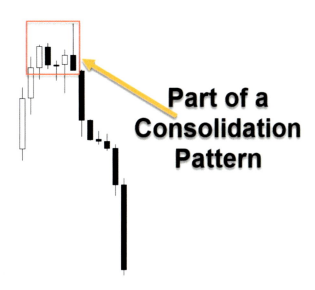

Part of a Consolidation Pattern

Figure 32. No longer lonely: Shooting Star as a part
of a sideways movement group

Shooting stars and hammers that are a part of a group can be found
either as a finisher candle, but sometimes they are right in the
middle. Either way, these candles always have a longish wick,
indicating buyers/sellers have stepped in aggressively. However, what
makes them more relevant as a part of a consolidating pattern is that
the sideways movement indicates the price has already stopped moving
in the same direction. Therefore, having a strong wick on the chart
means that the attempt at taking the price further in the same
direction has failed, with price spending a lot of time at the same
level.

Time is a huge component of trading. When I was a new trader, I had
heard about this concept but didn't quite understand what it meant.
It wasn't until I started using Market Profile that I managed to
grasp this simple truth: the longer the price spends at a particular
level, the greater the chances of that area acting as a reversal.

What we're doing is simply trying to identify those areas by reading what is already on the chart and not guessing what will happen. Traders are literally like detectives – you make deductions based on the evidence presented after doing due dilligence of the levels, across multiple timeframes.

It's perfectly okay to have an idea of what SHOULD happen around a certain level, but then we must WAIT for the right candle pattern to appear that speaks with the direction of your trading idea.

When I started using Market Profile, I quickly learned that once the market has started to print three 'TPOs' it means it's building structure at the level, potentially building a sideways movement. Once you've noticed that the price has stayed at the same price for several candles, it means there is no interest in taking it further. But this behaviour always must happen during the Regular Trading Hours if you're trading from the lower timeframes.

Three Inside Up/Down Pattern

One of the patterns that I see quite a lot but one that is rarely talked about is the Three Inside pattern. It comes in a couple of variations:

Three Inside Down | Three Outside Down

Three Inside Up | Three Inside Up

As the name says, it's a three-candle pattern which kind of looks like the morning/evening star. The main difference is in the middle candle, which doesn't have to be an 'indecision, neutral' candle.

Certain versions of this pattern are also called 'piercing line' for the bullish pattern and 'dark cloud cover' for the bearish version. However, these are usually found in stocks where the market closes overnight and the price opens lower or higher than the previous day's candle.

It's the only pattern in this book there you are actually entering the trade before the entire pattern is finished. In this regard, you are actually using a two-candle pattern called 'inside bar' to enter.

Inside bar has a simple rule when it comes to the strength of the pattern. The inside bar is only considered valid if the 2nd candle closes above the 50% of the entire length of the 1st candle:

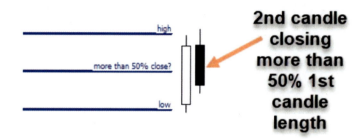

Figure 33. Basic rule for validity of the inside bar pattern

But in our algorithmic tests we determined that the inside bar is best used when the first candle was a much larger, abnormal sized candle. In most cases, the inside bar will probably be a start of a consolidation. As such it's not as safe to trade it just by the fact that an inside bar has appeared. A stronger option is always either an engulfing or a consolidating pattern. However, in certain cases it is acceptable to use the inside bar as a reversal pattern. If you're trading intraday, this would mean that you can use the inside bar to enter a trade at the correct time of day, especially in absence of any stronger patterns. One such valid scenario would be:

1. Exhausted Daily Range

2. Time of day is post option expiry

3. Inside bar appears

If you're trading from larger timeframes entering a trade on the basis of inside bar would need to be coupled with a larger-than-average first candle and a relevant swing extreme area. Otherwise, inside bars will have a high rate of failure.

Ideally the inside bar will eventually turn into a Three Inside/Outside pattern - where the third candle brings a good movement in the opposing direction that you've been looking for.

In that respect, Three Inside/Outside is the only pattern where you will be entering the trade on the basis on the inside bar, using other technical analysis techniques to determine whether this is a valid assumption. In this case, your exit would ideally be planned once the third candle brings you a strong move in the right direction. Once the third candle reaches at least 2:1 reward/risk ratio, the trade will be closed.

There is another thing to keep in mindL

Once all three candles have printed, the Three Inside/Outside pattern is usually not tradeable as a pullback from the 2nd candle close due to a high failure rate.

The pattern looks like this:

Figure 34. Three Inside Down - middle candle is inside the first candle length. Third candle goes well below the first candle close in ideal situations

The variations mostly pertain to whether the middle candle is inside the first candle's length or outside of it – sometimes referred to as 'dark cloud cover' – it's a similar pattern but you won't see this pattern much in forex or commodities because these markets run 24/5 leaving less chance for gaps. However this is what a stock version would like:

**Figure 35. Three Outside Down aka Dark Cloud Cover –
middle candle opened outside of 1st candle**

Sometimes this stock pattern can even look like an engulfing pattern if the 2nd candle goes all the way in the opposing direction:

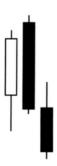

**Figure 36. 2nd candle turns into a bearish engulfing,
but this is still Three Outside Down pattern – although it can be treated
as an engulfing**

Same pattern variation is found when the middle candle high/low goes creates a new low/high in relation to the 1st candle. Here is an example of a bullish version of the pattern:

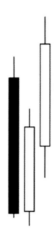

**Figure 37. Three Outside Up pattern –
middle candle made a new low before turning**

Rules For Trading Inside/Outside Patterns

I mentioned there's a bit of a problem with these pattterns if you want to trade reversals. The problem is that you have to enter upon the finish of the 2nd candle (inside bar) and then hope you're right on the third one for the follow-through.

The finish of the third candle move is also a rule for your trade exit. I usually have an issue with patterns where you need to guess before the pattern is 'whole'.

One simple rule for trading these as reversal is this:

The second candle close price has to be over 50% of the entire length of the 1st candle. Without this rule, entering Inside/Outside pattern in the forex and CFD markets will have a very high failure rate.

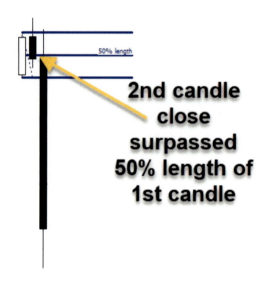

50% length

2nd candle close surpassed 50% length of 1st candle

Figure 38. Valid entry from a 2nd candle pattern.
Exit the trade after the 3rd candle finishes

The way I like to enter my trades is through a pullback to a newly formed candle pattern. I call this the 'Second Chance' entry. I use the 2nd chance entry for most price action patterns, however historically I found that if I missed the initial entry after the 2nd candle has finished, if the price pulls back to the originating area where the other party took control, these patterns have a high failure rate.

Therefore, if you've missed the entry from the 2nd candle, the only saving grace would be to flip to a higher timeframe and perhaps wait for an engulfing pattern to form. That is the second way to use these patterns.

I mentioned the Timeframe Intermix technique before, which involves flipping between different timeframes for clues and better decision making.

The way this would work for Three Inside/Outside is to spot this pattern on a low timeframe, third candle and all but then waiting for a larger timeframe to form a more solid pattern different that Three Inside/Outside. It's entirely possible to see a Three Inside/Outside pattern on the low timeframe, get a decent follow through on the third candle but unless the move continues and eventually shows up on a larger timeframe, then Three Inside/Outside has a high probability of failure. This is especially true when the third candle has quite a large follow-through.

Another use is exactly the opposite of this. If a small time frame creates a different strong pattern such as engulfing then you'd enter the small timeframe trade with a corresponding small stop loss but then continue to monitor a slightly higher timeframe for Three Inside/Outside creation.

For example:

- You use a 5 minute bullish engulfing to enter a trade

- You then flip to a 30 min chart to wait for the 2nd candle to close above the 50% of the first candle.

- If that happens, you can then plan the exit at the end of the third candle on the same 30 min chart. This is because you are now using the pattern mainly for monitoring the trade you're already in on.

Typically, this tends to happen when there was a massive large timeframe candle after some big news that brings me an opportunity for a somewhat quick mean-reversion trade which lasts a couple of hours at most. In this case, once again expecting a bullish engulfing is not a likely outcome. So I go to a 5 minute chart and look for a bullish engulf or consolidation and then I watch 30min or H1 chart for the creation of Three Inside/Outside. Once the candle has printed the third candle in the pattern, that's my exit rule.

Once again - if you've missed the clue for the 2nd candle entry and 50% rule relation to 1st candle, I would advise you to flip to a higher timeframe and monitor for another pattern to form. If you plan to use Three Inside/Outside to enter a trade after it forms all three candles, here are the pitfalls:

1. You'd be entering very late - at the top of the 3rd candle. You may get a gradual move on the third candle rather than a massive one, but that brings me to the second problem;

2. You'd have to use a much larger stop loss than necessary bringing you risk/reward ratio to 1:1 or less (which is the worst thing you can do in trading);

3. You're then asking for the market to give you another massive follow-through candle that jumps away even further than the one that created the third candle in the Three Inside/Outside pattern.

This kind of poor entry strategy may have worked in the 80s and 90s when the momentums resulted in huge moves in the forex markets but certainly not today where a move of even a 400 pip in one day is seldom found.

Look at it this way: not only has the market already had one abnormal move by (usually) creating a large 1st candle, but you're now asking it to create another abnormal move so that you could profit from it. Whilst not impossible, this happens extremely rarely - you simply cannot expect a complete retracement and a new high/low in the opposing direction very frequently. I prefer to rely on the norms in the market, rather than events that happen once in a blue moon.

To reiterate why I exit at the end of the 3rd candle: it's because follow-through on the 4th candle happens rarely.

I would also like to repeat once again that if the market retraces back to the 2nd candle close price, it is my experience that this pattern will fail. This observation of mine is now also supported by one of our in-house price action algorithms that measures price pattern reversal accuracy combined with my Q Points method. The pullback entry had a 12% success rate, meaning you'd need a consistent 10-12x reward/risk on the trades to make this profitable. Trading with 12% accuracy is painful, frustrating and would shake up the self-esteem of even the most confident trader.

Harami aka Inside Bar

I want to give some importance to the Harami pattern aka the inside bar. Although it's really not my favourite pattern to trade from, primarily because it's quite rare, Harami can be useful for early entries into the market.

Harami is a two candle pattern, where the 2nd candle is contained inside the body of the previous candle. It looks like this on the chart:

Figure 39. Second candle is much smaller and must be contained inside the body of the 1st candle

With the Harami pattern, I prefer to only trade it at the correct time of day. There are set times of day when the market likes to reverse intraday due to either a large option expiry, another exchange open (aka NYMEX or COMEX) or rebalancing the banks' portfolios for the end of day, all of which can cause an intraday trend reversal. How relevant these intraday reversals are, will depend on where they happen in relation to the large timeframe picture, the Bird's Eye view.

The only time you wouldn't need to consider time of day for accuracy is if you are trading from a Daily chart setting up a swing trade.

But still there a few issues to keep in mind in case your 1st reference candle for a Harami pattern was an abnormally large day, usually due to some unexpected fundamental release or news that caused the market to reprice.

On the other hand, having an abnormally large daily range for the previous candle definitely justifies going into a 'mean reversion' trade even before the harami has printed. To me, statistically, this indicates that the outlier that caused the abnormal day is no longer in focus and I am expecting the market to go back to its usual daily range. I would use a lower timeframe such as 4 Hour charts, 1 Hour and 30 min to look for my trade. But in case you missed this, should the day end with a Harami, it can be an early start of a reversal.

Statistically, outliers are a nightmare for most trading systems, however when you are using realtime price action, they are actually a very valuable opportunity for a mean reversion trade. This is exactly the case where a pattern such as Harami has a great chance to succeed.

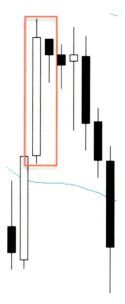

Figure 40. Harami pattern at the top of the move

Although the Harami pattern is useful to know about, I must say that Harami is quite a rare pattern in forex and CFD products. Unlike the other patterns in this book, you will not come across it day-to-day. I was hesitant to even include it in this book at all. If you go to any chart right now, you'll have to spend quite a while looking for a Harami. But once in a blue moon when they do appear, especially on the Daily chart on regular trading days (not Sundays) they are definitely a good way to enter a large reward/low risk trade to the opposing side. This is because the idea behind Harami patterns is that the side that was in control up until that point has lost all power indicating indecision, resulting in a much smaller candle than usual for the regular trading day.

I advise against using Harami patterns on intraday timeframes such as 5 min up to 1 hour charts. I myself found Harami largely unreliable for intraday trading, mostly because Harami relies on a previous candle size to determine how pathetic the Harami candle is. But sadly, there is no easy way for a human to quickly determine whether the candle that preceeded the Harami was an outlier or just a regular intraday move. Without this piece of information, trading Harami patterns intraday is not advised.

Double Tops and Double Bottoms

The next pattern I want to mention is the one and only pattern that is a cross between a chart pattern and a candle pattern.

The main reason why I find this useful in real-world trading is because it represents a sideways movement of sorts.

In a way, if the double top/double bottom occurs within a short number of candles, it does signify that the market has either topped out or bottomed out.

It's a pattern I most frequently found during the open at London session for forex pairs. I used it on 15min and 30min charts.

Here is what the pattern may look like:

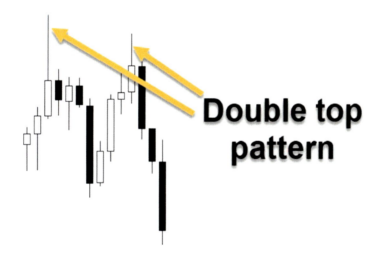

Figure 41. Double top reversal - pullback into previous consolidation

This chart pattern, if you analyse it well, is really a couple of candlestick patterns I previously wrote about.

In the above example there is a consolidation pattern which causes an initial move downwards. So by all accounts if you were awake to spot this you'd be in on the pattern long before the double top appears.

When the price tests a larger area of Supply/Demand for the first time, usually there's an initial move away on the lower timeframes which is then followed by a return to the originating zone and finally the 'real move'.

In Figure 40. Price goes back to the same area and tries to go higher but ultimately creates a strong bearish engulfing. This would give you the second entry opportunity.

When the bearish engulfing appears on the chart, you can also see that there's is a double top formed. This could be a signal to either add onto your position if you entered the trade with less of a size due to a shakey consolidation pattern.

Alternatively, if you missed the entry the first time around, you can now enter the market with some confidence that the initial reversal is still bringing the sellers to the party because you're not only seeing the double top, but also seeing a bearish engulfing.

Obviously with chart patterns there can be a million variations in regards to the types of initial reversals you'll notice.

You can either see the consolidation like the example above, or you can even have two engulfing patterns around the same area. You could have meandering prices that don't have a definable candlestick pattern

There is definitely a huge ambiguity when using chart patterns which is the main reason why I really dislike them but I still find the double tops/bottoms quite useful, especially if I've missed the clue the first time. Or if the first pattern happened at the 'wrong' time of day, ie during lunchtime when there's typically a lot of noise and fakeouts.

Double tops and double bottoms will happen fairly frequently in the market. They are also the main reason why the crowd who uses trailing stops to "protect" their trades get knocked out for scratch and then watch the price take off without them on board, despite the trader having identified the opportunity. Nothing worse for a trader – being right on the direction and not profiting from it.

The market loves pullbacks. In fact, when you first enter a trade, even after the initial move away, you will find that a lot of the times the price will come back to test the area where the move first originated from. Especially on lower timeframes. This is a completely normal market behaviour, across any asset class you may be looking at. I won't go too deep into the roles of 'Market Makers' vs 'Other Timeframe Participants' in this book, but let's just say that the **M**arket **M**akers (MMs) job is to provide the best possible price for **O**ther **T**imeframe **P**articipants (OTPs). Inexperienced traders blame the MMs for their lost trades but in reality, it's the inexperience and lack of knowledge that it the true cause and not the MMs.

MMs will use their buying/selling power to move the market up or down to the nearest deep liquidity pool so that the OTPs can execute their huge orders for institutional clients positions and portfolio management. These positions frequently go into hundreds of millions in unleveraged position size, equating to about 1,000 standard lots. I've seen them do 5,000 lots in thick markets such as S&P500 and eurusd.

But most noob retail traders trade out of fear. In an effort to mistakenly 'preserve' capital, they are frequently taken out of the market by these pullbacks into levels that the price had tested, moved away and then tested again.

So before you go placing your trailing stops (I am generally against them), ensure that the market has tested the originating area already.

You are then in a safer, stronger position to protect your trading capital. A much better way to control your risk is through 'partialling' trades once they reach a minimum 2x reward/risk.

1. Allow the trade to reach 2x r/r

2. Cut it in half

You are then sitting on a net/net 0% risk trade to your account and yet still having the opportunity to make profits should the market continue in the same direction.

If you find most of your trades even reach 3x r/r, then you can afford to only cut a third and still stay in a large enough position with all the upside and zero risk without any compromise to your original zone and original stop loss placement.

Moving your stop too soon to break even (or 'scratch') is a very rookie mistake. Sure I've been there and done that in the beginning, but in my decade of trading I am confident in my trade entry choices without the need to resort to trailing stops. Once you have years of consistent trading to analyse, you may come to the same conclusion as me: I will rather lose a trade than move it to scratch, only to see the market go in the direction I was speculating on.

To use the words of one of my traders Yana P. who tragically lost her life to an aggressive form of stomach cancer at only 29 years age:

"It hurts me more to not be in a trade that I was correct on than to get knocked out when I'm wrong!".

Pullback Entry Technique
(Second Chance Entry)

For the final chapter in this short study of candlestick patterns, I would like to share my favourite entry technique.

I am known for my fairly accurate early entries into the market because of one thing: I am extremely good at recognising the price pattern in realtime and exceptionally good at pullback entries into those price patterns.

I call this technique the Second Chance Entry because it relies on a price pullback into the candle pattern at a very particular key price level. Simply speaking, the key level for my entry will always be the common price point where the market created an equilibrium.
For the 2-candle patterns this is always the open of the previous candle. I refer to this 'common price point' as the 'conterminous line'.

You will hear me harp on about the conterminous line on our Market Stalkers Youtube channel quite a bit. So now you know what it means!

What does this conterminous line look like on the chart?

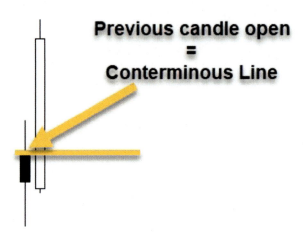

**Figure 42. Conterminous line is a common price point
at the time of price reversing direction and my choice of entry**

Keeping in mind this market behaviour, as you begin to see the price movement with new eyes, you will start noticing the following behaviour:

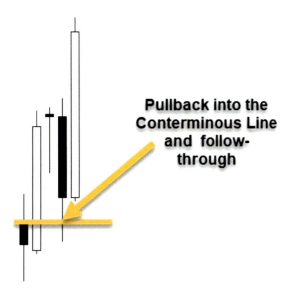

Figure 43. After the pullback, the market carries on in the new direction

Instead of entering the market immediately upon the engulfing
candlestick pattern finishing, I wait for the market to test the newly
formed 'demand' area. Most new traders are extremely afraid of
entering the market upon this kind of pullback, because it's scary –
but I've tested this technique over a decade during the most turbulent
market conditions the world has ever seen. And quite simply – it
works.

The Second Chance Entry enables you to enter the market with a lot
less risk, saving quite a few pips/ticks and reducing risk of a large
drawdown.

Some old-school traders may wait for a low of the pattern to enter
however this frequently results in breaking and invalidating the
entire pattern in the first place. I was always incredibly
uncomfortable with this.

If the pattern I based my trading idea on is no longer there because the market made a new low/high - is my idea still valid?

Absolutely not!

I am highly against trading absolute lows and highs unless you're referencing a higher timeframe supply/demand area, where another high/low is still holding. But even then, I prefer to trade reactions that result from these larger areas, rather than guess that they will be 'reactive'. We cannot predict the market. But we can speculate about what should happen and then wait for the price action to show us whether we're correct or not. That is the true meaning of 'trading the chart and not your bias'. In simple terms: no price action, no trade!

No crazy trading, no guesswork - just a methodical way to find your trade direction and then a systematic entry technique to obtain your position.

Second Chance Entry works for Consolidation Patterns too. However the conterminous line will be related to the finisher engulfing candle rather than the start of the entire sideways movement. So once the finisher candle is done and dusted you will have the conterminous line.

Second Chance Entry works for Morning/Evening Stars as well. The middle candle open is the conterminous line.

Here are a some more examples of where the conteminous line is located:

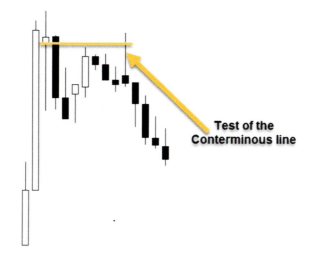

Figure 44. Evening Star Pattern and 2nd Chance Entry

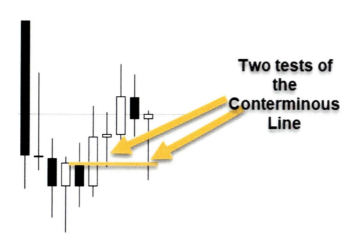

Figure 45. Consolidation Pattern and Entry Area

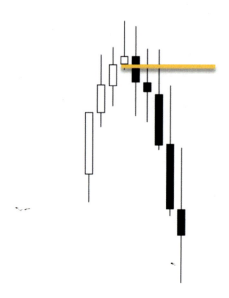

Figure 46. Bearish Engulfing Conterminous Line Entry

- End of Chapter 5 -

Q Points

My book wouldn't be complete if I didn't mention my own proprietary method of finding trade locations: Q Points aka Quartile Points.

Although I started my journey as a supply/demand trader with scoring the zones, placing limit orders at my zones of interest etc, over the years I started to notice that market would turn at areas high/low enough in the overall established swing. Sometimes even well before it reached an S/D zone. And sometimes even at 'weak' S/D zones.

I began to journal through these events. After a few years I had an epiphany during a release of a Q3 for stocks - I was running an ex-dividend capture strategy for a week ahead of the release along with shorting the stock on the day in the cash markets. As I was doing my market prep Ransquawk were yapping on about quarterly numbers. I thought to myself: I wonder if simplifying S/D by breaking down the swing into simple quarters would work?

So I drew these lines using a modified Fib tool to display quarters automatically and over the next year I watched and journalled my observations. Sure enough, market seemed to react from 'Q Points' as they became known later and they were a wonderfully simple way to weed out S/D zones that are not relevant. When Blahtech acquired my company Angelo Capital, we started work on our now very popular Blahtech SD indicator. During this project we developed further conditions of when a Q Point is relevant and also redefined what makes a Q Point in the first place. Suffice to say that the default setting in the Blahtech SD was the one that yielded the most consistent results in the algorithm tests using Q Points.

Scoring of the zones also becomes a little less relevant when you're using Q Points with immediate price action pattern around the Q Point or/and the zone you wish to trade from.

Rather than relying on a limit order, I prefer waiting for one of the price patterns described in this book to show up first on a lower timeframe. These days I rarely use limit orders. On occasion I will use them to get into a trade from a conterminous line test, but I've completely stopped using them to 'guess' if an S/D zone might work upon the first test. Most of the time, this approach enables me to get into a trade for a fraction of a stop loss size. This is because I have no need to use the entire originating zone to trade, but rather using a reaction price pattern at the correct daytrading timezone (a concept described in my Level 2 Pro Development course). I modified this approach due to my career as a futures trader, where holding positions overnight was not an option. When I started with futures trading I was a profitable swing trader but I had trouble translating supply/demand into intraday. It took me about 3 years to discover and learn how to combine S/D, market profile, time of day and Average Daily Range exhaustions for maximum efficiency.

This process lead to an eventual creation of **Market Stalkers Professional Development Program** that I now have on the main Market Stalkers site. Few years ago, I was asked to work with junior traders as a part of my senior trader role. To maximise my time I started creating some basic videos, some of which are still on our youtube channel (search for Market Stalkers and subscribe). First few videos I made were unstructured with me just talking things through.

I wasn't happy bringing that to the public. I hold a Masters Degree in classical flute. When I was younger I used to teach music so I am well versed in the methodics of practice along with psychology of high level skill development.

Since I already enjoy teaching others, I decided to use my music teaching skills and apply it to trading. As such I wanted to create a highly structured course with progressive difficulty that can be easily digested, step-by-step.

I am fully aware that there are trader education companies who may look like they offer the same level of professional trading strategies (usually for the price of a new car) however one critisicm was that the other companies present the material in a chaotic way. Their lessons are done through a series of multi-hour webinars that wallpaper you with highly advanced concepts right from the opening sequence. But in order to learn how to run, we must learn to crawl and then walk. Which is why we took almost 2 years to create and tweak our Professional Development Courses. We are CPD-certified which means you can Market Stalkers Courses towards your professional development credits in certain countries such as UK.

If you're not already a Market Stalker and you wish to advance (or enhance) your trading skills by learning how we're generating profitability and consistency, the CPD-certified program description can be found here:

https://marketstalkers.thinkific.com

We aim to add value to the trader community but also to source out trader talent for our trading department by funding accounts of our best students based in UK and EU.

All interested Traders are required to run a Darwinex-based account which represents ther mini-fund for track record keeping. It also acts as an investor-enabled account, simplifying the whole idea of running a fund. They even provide you with tax returns.

If you're a USA resident, then funding is not possible with our company directly. In that case, please go to one of our partners. See this page for more details:
https://marketstalkers.thinkific.com/pages/funded-accounts

If your aim is to become a profitable independent trader, come and sign up as a free member on the main website to watch four complimentary lessons on the method.
You may even want to join our youtube channel and watch the bi-weekly videos (search for Market Stalkers).

- *The End* -

To watch my video course on candlestick patterns as a supplement to this book, please go to my Udemy course:

https://www.udemy.com/market-stalkers-candlestick-patterns-trading-analysis

Additional information:

Market Stalkers have developed our own unique suite of price action indicators thanks to a brilliant collaboration with our parent company Blahtech Limited. Blahtech developed Blahtech MP for MT5

specifically upon request from AMP Futures, one of the largest futures trading brokers in the USA.

Blahtech indicators for MT4 and MT5 can be found on MQL5.com Marketplace (search for Blahtech).

Links to the indicators can also be found here:

http://www.blahtech.co.uk/products

For our CPD-certified Professional Development Program that teaches you how to evaluate the market like a professional, using institutional order flow on large and small timeframes, please go to:

https://marketstalkers.thinkific.com

Made in the USA
Middletown, DE
26 April 2025

74769247R00044